THE POETRY COLLECTION ON LOVE

CHIRANJEET MISHRA

Made with ♥ on the Notion Press Platform
www.notionpress.com

These pieces are dedicated to all my exes and my loved ones.

Contents

1. A Glass Half Filled

I chased through the clouds
Bearing the scary thunderstorms
The sunrise seemed a fairytale
But, Hey your smile gave air to my sail.
You spent years in my dreams
Holding me closer than I
Ah! Only if you could
Love a little not just lie
Is it a harmony
Or are you just a Cuscuta
To my apple honeyed
the strong and sturdy Quercus Texana.
Are we the cherry blossoms in Spring
Or Winter's frosty brittled branch n leaves
I hope for neither
Rather a weather colder yet sweeter than these.

2. Happiness

Today, a day like no other
Yet akin to each of mine
Stabs the same wounds, not clever
Happiness a poison, say just fine
A secret scent thickly forlorn
Engulfs my lungs cigarly
Death a mercy, life a misery
Burdened me, snapped fervently
Loves & cares my heart for naught
As if forged of lead
An eternal sickness makes me oft
Forget the need of dread
My song a mummers farce
Lies ingrained oceanly
Truth, a drop of ink
Do I 'exist' merely?
Bid me farewell
I beg my worries eternally
Drowning me it pays no heed
Tends to my Fire of Misery...

3. An Unspoken Desire

Hazed and blurred reminiscences
Translates to mournful joy to I
Colorless flowers bloom and wither
Akin 'We' did to 'You' and 'I'
Damned be my doting heart
A fool to your eternal charisma
Overwhelmed by thine witchery
I turned into fragile crockery
Woe that clouds
Wringing the neck of my life
Shall make I doubt
Arth you an illusioned fantasy?
Trusting thine leonine strength
For nonce and for ever
Let thee hold my palpitant segment
Condemning me your paramour...

4. The Lament Unheard

Throes that kept bounding, fields
Which cradled my hope-seeds
Breathing under the burden breeze
To day's eyes or roses with finesse
Interwoven were our temperate feathers
That kept away the harsh weather
Say a binary system in ether
Which fall into each other yet forever
Blunder of mine it was
To veil the creeks and cracks
Unnoticed & uncared they grew
Apart to a million miles & a few
Had it been a waste?
Ponders my heart with unreined haste
Fruitless attempts at defining us
Shall only lead me to carcass and dust
Like the Phoenix that burns it's funeral pyre
Rise I shall free of solicitudes & desires...

5. Ode To Beauty

Hues from the spectrum I lost
As a days span was stretched eternally
Reason I cannot else I be frost
With the melancholy that bodes my day cloudy
My eyes mimic the shadiest cloud
My heart bleeds to lead
I write and beseech no response
Shivers my hand for the dread of loss
Humble I was & revere I do
For earnest I am & without further ado
I hope to unite, althooh
Patience of immortality I hold for you
Thee arth my Endymion
I be your Selene
Time be our Zeus
And your love be my co-ca-ne .

6. Fates

Treacherous fingers entangle strings
Strings that puppet ye beings
Twisting and turning every way
Bringing forth blissful dismay
Shrieks my harth to reason
Not to care & clear my vision
To remain stone, nay falter down
And pay no heed to sapphire beauty found
A voice deep, in my slumber
Tugs me towards the dreaded end
Like mindless sheep I follow
The tune of the Fate's fluty wallow
Tendrils crawl the rusted gates
That were locked ages ago
The land wasting and breeding undergrowth
Receives the touch of a fay's soul
Dull senses, yet I drain opiates
Carefree and Careless
Just a tad betwixt them
Wouldst it be long ere Lethe I drank?...

7. A Separation's Ease Parchment

Longings I bear for ought I have,
Wilfully the path of today walked upon,
Fears I had were unclothed of me,
Standing vulnerable & naked viz a newborn.
Like the frozen peaks that melt by drop,
That drop I am in search of another,
The another being you, miles afar yet together,
Naught in dismay, naught in despair
Just the dear hope, trust and eclair-affair.
Travelled I have through the brook,
That sings its melody immensely sweet,
Its course uncertain and unpredictable,
brought growth and crucified many a feat.
Through curtains & veils were we disclosed,
To ourselves of past & humble morrow,
Memories we created quite a few
Imprinted on thine-my soul evermore
Through patience and faith but nay regretful sorrow.
Tarry we cannot, nay should be bound,
Of empty promises & far-off desires,
But I must confess a truth too harsh,
Fairy tales be false as be pain-bereft love,

'To', being in ourselves' hearts, a flame that never grows cold...

'To', being in ourselves' hearts, a flame that never grows cold...

8. The Unsaid Regrets

Her demeanour unfathomable & ubiquitous beguils
Have my palpitant segment
Flutter like the sapphirine hummings
Opiates stir no strings
I, be a hooligan to thee
Numero Uno! Has she known tad-beneath?
Shall I speak dexterously my myriad of sins?
Can she not abhor I and perceive akin?
Obstructed by oneself's hurdles & pitfalls
The thought's wings clipped & word's lamed
I cut my thread-affinity & bricked my walls
Having incentivised to never reminisce erst-
faded
How foolish to commit such blunders
how craven to admit my faults
Despair and forlorn my sworn brothers
Lost I am, until death I crawl

9. Why Oh Proclivity Be My Guest

Rise I not with the sun
But rise I do with a thought
How beautiful she looks I fawn
Contemplate she cannot the urge I fought
Affection could be the illusion
Veiled by her pheromones
Dilate my pupils do
Drought voice finds infusion
Every encounter mums the ambience
Frames of glass we build under curtains
Holding together I concrete them
Betwixt thee and I it remains
Swear I can to protect them eternally
Trust I do and love thee more
Risked I have for vulnerable be my heart's core
Stab you can or lend me yours
Betwixt and between, I shall leave without remorse.

10. The Beck Of My Existence

Possibilities of the impossible
Overpowered my sense of reason
Anticipation and sanguiness flamed my desire
Since the moment you marked our journey
So ignorant I was to feel that passion
Unknown to the symptoms of being in love
My desperate and shy convinced me
To have the affection of a friend
Than lose you forever
Happiness engulfed me leaving only a spark of dissatisfaction
You helped break my boundaries
For I was just another open book
In ink I confessed my fallacies
Scared of being rejected and forgotten
I dreaded my nightmares of daylight
Being smart and knowing me better than I
You chose silence than any other reply
I accepted the fruitless attempt but grieved no less
You grew distant to protect me?
Falling apart as we were
How I erred! And regret what followed
You are a canoe in the beck of my life

Flow treacherous and deadlier than most
Shall we survive this distant journey?
With just you as the oars of my soul
~ T.T.M.

11. To A Princess

Beauty that even the goddess
Looks at and burns with jealousy
I hope you could only imagine
the state of my mortal sight
Hair braided so blissfully
Your body bereft of ornaments
Just this sight strums strings
That even divinity could not
My fantasies include only one
The one who holds my heart
One whom i could never have fathomed
Nor my vocabulary would suffice to describe
Asphodels of my life recede away
My being breathes only for you
Wishing we could be more than
I, an admirer and you personification of love.

12. Avatar Of Death

Dark clouds, yet the moon
Shone brightly all alone
Carelessly I shed my skin
In an attempt to find my kin
Cursed with a sickness
Not of the mortal realm
How terrible! How perilous!
Death, that's what she was to men.
Desperate to breathe her scent
My heart would only lament
For it was all just a farce
Deceived I was! What an illusion she cast!
Fading I am into the abyss
Falling deeper! Oh what a bliss
Seeming akin a harmless kiss
Ah! She was blessed with Death's lips.

13. A Heartbroken Bard

The fracture of his heart
Resonated within this bard
Singing to the melancholy
For his death could no longer tarry
It took his all not to scream
Was everything just one of her schemes?
It took his all to not fall dead
With the swiftest thud, bereft of breath.
He smiled the brightest he ever had
He looked amused! Oh the poor lad!
Laughing his way through the pain
He wondered, "Was it all in vain?"
Tears streamed down his cheeks
For his sense of reason had ceased
'HIS' motives were never more amiss
Taking a leap, he gave Death a kiss.

14. Silence

Silence is a dream
Oh! so clear and pristine
Fresh as the juiciest plums
Skin bereft of any bumps.
Silence is a prison
For Men, without reason
She binds us with fears
Fear of isolation and friendless tears.
Ah! Is she the darkness within me?
Or am I within her darkness?
Contemplate he cannot, this being called me,
For Silence is beyond an ego's awareness.
She speaks to this broken heart
As if defying herself
She tells me to be a famous bard
A dream I never had myself.
She's consuming me, falling to the ground,
Think I cannot, scared to make a sound
Drawing me closer to her lips
Silence bestows an eternal sleeps kiss.

15. Autumn Leaves

We used to talk about the stars in the sky
Talk about the love in our eyes
The memories veiled
By the tough choices we made.
Now we both walk by
Unhindered by the sparks of love
Silence our only vocabulary
Even a touch as rare as a Golden Spree
Distance between us seems million-fold
My subconscious sensing your every move
Whenever we lock eyes
It doesn't take a billionth of a second to flinch
Oh! How easily perfect it seemed
Hugs, kisses, cuddles, & us intertwined
We fell so fast
As if we were leaves in the fall
Now i see lilies blooming around you
Butterflies that drink from your sweetness
I wish we had tried some more
I wish it were Summer & we were still in love.

ore.

16. Sleepless Nights

Farewell to this shattered heart
I wished with all mine might
Yet despair and forlorn found infusion
Overtaking all the senses you may find.
Being a vessel that cannot contain,
Being one's true hateful self
Oh! how I wish to be reborn anew
Oh! how I regret my blasphemy.
Do my promises hold no value now?
Am I a mere puppet to her will?
Oh! How mortal I have become
Isn't there a way to break the seal?
Bloody wars may not make me cower
But silence a weapon she chose
Even Gods fail to breathe without fear
This cold stare, oh how quickly I froze.
Love I do and shall cherish you forever
This foolish bard wishes no more
Only to burn in this agonising fever,
Until the day we are sung as a folklore.

17. Voyager Vanquisgh

Trod have none on this land
Sailed across the ocean one manned,
Grass emerald, Sky azure,
How could be someone's heart so pure.
Eyes obsidian, hair dark as midnight
Flesh and skin the hue of Citrine
Voice of Nightingale under the twilight
Her soul so clear and pristine.
Darkness shrouding me in fear
Desolation a being very near
Her Psyche be my candle light
Burning gaudily with Sun's might
The perfume I smell be her pheromones
Tranced she has, I with a drooling fantasy,
Act I have with razing hormones
Committed none but many a fallacy.
Arms around each other with a promise of forever,
Pinions keeping us warm in this icy weather
Our lips touched, yet not, can they bid adieu ever?
Countable will be the stars but our kisses will outnumber.

18. A Day Spent Without You

Welcome to this lament of mine
Indeed, I am in pain and decline
Sorrow enshrouding my star sign
Melancholic yearning, I bear for thine.
Time a concept that eludes comprehension,
Distance a barrier that denies reduction,
How dreadful and teary be my situation,
Can even He find me a solution?
Hurt you had this foolish bard
Weaken I did and left you charred
Mend we can one another's heart
Fill every void with each other's shard.
Truth be told a day is not eternity
Though believe I cannot with certainty
Wait I shall with fear for sempiternity,
Farewell reader for the sake of brevity.

19. Question A Lost Soul Asks

In some dream, you were conjured

From memories, with you, I forged,

It seems you are a pixie,

Crafted by Him from stardust.

Wings grew from my back

Dreams of the sky grew within me

But how could I let go of this earthly sack

Crawling, a reality, can I ever flee?

Should I despair?

Should I lose hope?

Can I not fight fair?

Can I not keep away this rope?

Pondering these questions I walk forward,

Until the end of time, I am lost,

A crack in me, she turned it into the abyss,

That I fall into, my soul covered in frost.

20. A Vanquished Heart

The sky seems to ask me something
Something I know I can't say
Because my heart would deny beating
If I accept the bitter truth of today
I feel like a lonely dark cloud
Alone and depressed in this world
When will I stop crying out loud?
When will I hit the right chord?
I make you cry; I make you sad
Why am I alive ponders this lad,
I feel unworthy of you; I feel useless,
Why do you need me? Even I am clueless.
You asked if we are falling apart
You asked if I love you at all
Your crushes hit like a poisonous dart
You treat me like, I can be a missed call.
I want to change myself
I want to fight for you
I am trying my best without any help
But you don't acknowledge my efforts for you
You think no one's here for you
Maybe you are right
Maybe I shouldn't exist in your life
Cause all I do is hurt you and hurt you.

I wish I died before I met you
I wish I didn't make you fall in love with me
I wish all of this wasn't true
I wish you didn't have any memories of me
Can I please turn back time
To relish the good old days
To fix these past mistakes of mine
Just to see a smile on your face.

21. The Untamed Wildness

Her soul's essence belongs to the Moon
Her aura to the blazing Sun
Her composure calm as the midnight
Her complexion more chocolate than cream
Vibrations of these uncharted lands
Channel through my heart's magic wand
Oh! How the hymns felt so bland
My eyes blind to your wavelength band
Those mysterious and silent eyes
Restraining any deduction attempt of mine
The truth hidden better than any lie
Was it her innocence or her poisoned wine
Not a moment passes by
That i don't repent and cry
Even if I try to justify
But she doesn't want to try
Every ounce of emotion that we shared
Was it a dream or art you prepared
Seconds turn into hours, hours into days
Alas! I fear I shall be lost forever in this maze.
My patience challenged by the Gods
Shall I prevail against all odds?
Those pouted lips and breasts i fawn
The dark eyes that reveal all but none.

22. A Fresh Start

Simple it was for you
To say those last few words
Easy it was to forget
I don't even strum anymore chords
You sent me away
Far away in this lonely world
To fight alone
With just a broken sword
Flashes of my beloved
Reminiscing of the past
How much longer
Shall this wretched day last?
Care and love seem like poison
As if of hemlock I have drunk
Hatred and anger be two emotions
This heart can't feel even if its sunk
Everyday a new beginning
A new beginning without you
Without you I move forward
I move forward in this darkness
In this darkness I try to breathe
I try to breathe everyday

23. A Fated Encounter

While I was in the darkness
While I was falling deeper
You introduced me to happiness
Bringing back this lost lover
Days and weeks pass by
Flashes of past don't forget to haunt
You care and love when I cry
Turning into memories I can flaunt
Tapestries new but the art ancient
On handlooms we knit unbeknownst to us
A promise to keep it all a secret
An oath to take it to the grave of us
Promised I had to not feel again
Promised to have a heart of lead
Sense it makes naught for you to bargain
Because this heartless bard is brimming with dread
Oh! What a liar I am?
Oh! How weak be my resolve?
These palpitations I feel such a sham!
A very treacherous riddle to solve!
Only ponder and question I shall
This fated encounter of mine
None know what the future shall
Hold in its glass of wine

24. Waiting

Wait I shall for years to come
Just to see that lovely smile
Wait I shall till the end of time
Loving and caring for you all that while
Your eyes dark as midnight
Your hair blacker than death
Your lips! Oh such a juicy sight!
Your breasts took away my breath
Time spent together brought us closer
Scared to say 'I love you', Afraid 'us' shall become 'I' and 'You'
My love for you broke all barriers,my heart could not become any
more merrier
I started to live once again, i recieved your love without any
bargain.
The fear still has a remnant soul
Losing you , perhaps, you leaving me alone
I challenge the Gods to test us
To try with all their might to seperate us
Fail they shall every damn time
Cause this love is eternal , and their worth just a dime!

25. A Reminiscent Bard

Broken we were, separate from each other
Leave you did, breaking your promise of forever
My palpitations started to wither, as if it was winter
Light forgot about me, a black veil i hid under
Everytime I see you,my heart begs to stop
I wish I was blind, I wish I lost hope
I wish you happiness, I wish I could lie
I wish it would all end, I wish you stopped making me cry
I knew you would find someone else
Everyone told me it would hurt
As if I am any different or else
I would have a heart charred and burnt
They say time shall heal it all
They say to live in the present
How could I forget it all?
I even miss your seductive scent.